PETER PAN:
THE BOY WHO HATED MOTHERS
A play by Michael Lluberes

Based on "Peter and Wendy" by J.M. Barrie

PETER PAN: THE BOY WHO HATED MOTHERS was commissioned by No RulesTheatre Company. The world premiere was presented by No Rules Theatre Company, February 2012.

It was written in part at The Hambidge Center for Creative Arts and Sciences during a New Artist Initiative Residency sponsored by The National Endowment of the Arts.

PETER PAN: THE BOY WHO HATED MOTHERS
received its world premiere in February 2012, produced by
No Rules Theatre Company (Co-Artistic Directors Joshua
Morgan & Brian Sutow, Producing Director Anne S. Kohn).

The production was directed by Michael Lluberes, with
scenic design by Daniel Pinha, lighting design by Carrie
Wood, costume design by Brandon R. McWilliams, sound
design & original music by Elisheba Ittoop. The stage
manager was Theresa Hindersinn.

The cast was as follows:

PETER PAN.................................... John Evans Reese
WENDY DARLING JANE.....................Megan Graves
MRS. DARLING/CAPTAIN HOOK.............Lisa Hodsoll
/ADULT WENDY
JOHN DARLING........................... Joshua Rosenblum
TOOTLES/SMEE................................ Adam Downs
NIBS/BILL JUKES/TIGER LILY...............Maya Jackson
SLIGHTLY/STARKEY..................... Nathaniel Mendez

PETER PAN: THE BOY WHO HATED MOTHERS received its west coast premiere in April 2013, produced by The Blank Theatre (Artistic Director Daniel Henning).

The production was directed by Michael Matthews, with scenic design by Mary Hamrick, lighting design by Zack Lapinski and Tim Swiss, costume design by Kellsy MacKilligan and sound design by ReBecca Kessin. The stage manager was Rebecca Eisenberg. It was produced by Sarah Bauer and Stephen Moffatt.

The cast was as follows:

PETER PAN............................ Daniel Shawn Miller
WENDY DARLING/JANE......................... Liza Burns
MRS. DARLING/CAPTAIN HOOK/......... Trisha LaFache
/ADULT WENDY
JOHN DARLING..........................Benjamin Campbell
TOOTLES/SMEE...................... ....Jackson Evans
NIBS/BILL JUKES/TIGER LILY..............Amy Lawhorn
SLIGHTLY/STARKEY........................ David Hemphill

LICENSING & PRODUCTION INQUIRIES
Uproar Theatrics, LLC.
hello@uproartheatrics.com I www.UproarTheatrics.com

Peter Pan: The Boy Who Hated Mothers copyright © 2013
by Michael Lluberes

Peter Pan: The Boy Who Hated Mothers
is published by Uproar Theatrics, LLC
500 8th Ave FRNT 3, #1714 New York, NY 10018

ISBN: 978-1-968051-40-2

First Printing, March 2026

CAUTION: Professionals and amateurs are hereby warned that all material in this script and libretto, being fully protected under the copyright laws of the United States, the British Empire including the Dominion of Canada, and all other countries of the Copyright Union, is subject to royalty. All rights, including professional, amateur, motion picture, recitation, lecturing, public reading, radio and television broadcasting, and the rights of translation into foreign languages, are strictly reserved. The stock and amateur performance rights in the English language through the United States, its territories and possessions and the rest of the World are controlled exclusively by Uproar Theatrics, LLC., www.UproarTheatrics.com, 500 8th Ave FRNT 3 #1714 New York, NY 10018-4597 No performances of the play may be given without obtaining in advance the written permission of Uproar Theatrics, LLC. and paying the requisite fee. Inquiries concerning all other rights should be directed to Uproar Theatrics, LLC. at the web address stated above.

SPECIAL NOTE: Anyone receiving permission to produce Peter Pan: The Boy Who Hated Mothers is required to give credit to Michael Lluberes as sole and exclusive author of the Play on the title page of all programs distributed in connection with performances of the Play and in all instances in which the title of the Play appears, including printed or digital materials for advertising, publicizing or otherwise exploiting the Play and/or a production thereof. Please see your production license for font size and typeface requirements. It is the licensee's responsibility to ensure any and all required billing is included in the requisite places, per the terms of the license.

AUTHOR'S NOTE

When J.M. Barrie was six years old, his thirteen year old brother David died in an ice skating accident. His mother was devastated by David's death and found solace in the idea that by dying, her son would remain a little boy forever. From the depths of J.M. Barrie's own longing, he crafted a potent myth about childhood, loss and what it means to grow up.

The story of Peter Pan is a bloody battle and a delicate dance between children and adults. Barrie was exploring the terrain of a child's psychology and imagination in this work. The story is a beautiful allegory about the pain and inevitability of growing up. Using one of Barrie's own original titles: "The Boy Who Hated Mothers", some of his initial ideas for the play and his novelization of the story "Peter and Wendy", the hope of this adaptation is to unlock some of the darker mysteries buried deep inside his masterpiece.

"The horror of my boyhood was that I knew a time would come when I also must give up the games... This agony still returns to me in dreams... I felt that I must continue playing in secret." -J.M. Barrie

"There are two worlds, the world of everyday and the world of the imagination. When children play, they pass quite naturally through the two worlds all the time, so that at one moment a child may hold a stick and pretend it's a sword. At one moment you can tell him to drop that stick and he responds to that. At the same time you can tell him to drop that sword and he responds to that. The two worlds coexist. The theatre should be a meeting place between these two worlds." -Peter Brook

This new version of the story is a dangerous game of make believe, a dark exploration of the psyche of a child. Barrie created a theatrical playground of childhood memories, fears and imagination for the adult and child within each of us to play together.

"Cast your mind back into its earliest years, and through them you will see flitting dimly the elusive form of a child. He is yourself, as soon as you can catch him. But move a step nearer, and he is not there. Among the mists of infancy he plays hide and seek with you, until one day he trips and falls into the daylight. Now you seize him; and with that touch you two are one." -J.M. Barrie

Welcome to Neverland!

-Michael Lluberes

SETTING

London, 1904. The Darling nursery and inside a child's mind.

CHARACTERS/DOUBLING

PETER PAN - Male.
Haunting, otherworldly. Ageless magical boy. Physical, spontaneous. He still has his baby teeth, his first laugh. Aggressive, manic, emotional, impulsive, seductive. Has a strange power that draws everyone to him.

WENDY DARLING/JANE – Female.
[WENDY] Accent: RP British. Age 12. The heart of the play. At the edge of childhood, going through the beginning stages of puberty. Clever. Her mind and body are changing a lot. Also plays
[JANE] Accent: RP British. Age 10. Wendy's daughter. Curious and brave.

MRS. DARLING/CAPTAIN HOOK/ADULT WENDY - Female.
[MRS. DARLING] Accent: RP British. Mother of the Darling children. She used to be warm, graceful; the embodiment of motherhood but is so distraught by the death of her baby she's not able to function. Also plays
[HOOK] Accent: RP British. The greatest villain ever. Scary, elegant, mysterious, cold, theatrical, oily, bloodthirsty. The embodiment of a child's nightmare. Something of the Grand Guignol about him. Noel Coward mixed with Adolph Hitler. Also plays
[ADULT WENDY] Accent: RP British. "She was not a little girl heart-broken about him; she was a grown woman smiling at it all, but they were wet smiles."

JOHN DARLING - Male.
Accent: RP British. Age 10. Delicate, hypersensitive, highly intelligent, in danger of growing up to be the stereotypical buttoned up Englishman.

TOOTLES/SMEE - Male.
[TOOTLES] Accent: RP British. Lost boy. Could be chubby, small or round. Sensitive, funny, sweet, melancholic, soft, "poor kind Tootles, humblest of the boys. Quite the silliest one". Obsessed with mothers. The baby of the Lost Boys. Also plays
[SMEE] Accent: Cockney. Tootles' shadow. Hook's right hand man. Not cute and cuddly. He helps Hook murder children. Hook and Smee are like an old married couple. Has a mean streak as well.

NIBS/BILL JUKES/TIGER LILY- Female.
[NIBS] Accent: Northern Country. Lost boy. Strange. He has a special relationship with Tinker Bell, whom he communicates with for the others. Lots of secrets. Also plays
[BILL JUKES] Pirate. Nib's shadow. Also plays
[TIGER LILY] Young Indian princess of her tribe. Beautiful, brave, proud, strong.

SLIGHTLY/STARKEY - Male.
[SLIGHTLY] Accent: London Cockney. Lost boy. Know it all. A comedian. An improviser. Artful Dodger. A little conman. A chameleon. Scrappy. Funny. Also plays
[STARKEY] Pirate. Slightly's shadow.

ACT ONE

1. THE DREAMS OF CHILDREN

(Stars. Parts office an old Victorian nursery. Two beds, a crib, a dresser, a toy chest, a baby carriage, a chair, a rocking horse, a nursery wall with faded peeling wallpaper, a window, discarded broken children's toys. A group of actors emerge from the space. All except Peter. They are somewhere between children and adults. Are they dead? Are they the children from the story all grown up? They exist somewhere between asleep and awake. They look as if they've just woken up from a dream. Mrs. Darling pushes the baby carriage around the nursery. She discards the carriage, walks to an old toy chest and opens it.)

ALL

All children grow up.

MRS. DARLING

Except one.

SLIGHTLY

Peter Pan was said to live with the fairies.

NIBS

There were odd stories about him, as that when children died, he went part of the way with them, so they should not be frightened.

JOHN

Perhaps he was a little boy who died young, and this is how the author conceived his subsequent adventures.

TOOTLES
Perhaps he was a boy who was never born at all – a boy
whom some people longed for, but who never came.

MRS. DARLING
Perhaps you have seen him in the faces of women who have
no children.

WENDY
Perhaps you have seen him at *your* nursery window.

ALL
All children grow up.

MRS. DARLING
Except one.

       (Mrs. Darling closes the toy chest. Wendy and
       Mrs. Darling act out the following.)

WENDY
Children soon know that they will grow up, and the way
Wendy knew was this. One day when she was two years old
she was playing in a garden, and she plucked a flower and
ran with it to her mother. And Mrs. Darling put her hand to
her heart and cried:

MRS. DARLING
Oh, why can't you remain like this forever?

WENDY
And this was all that passed between them on the subject.
But henceforth Wendy knew that she must grow up. You
always know after you are two.

ALL
Two is the beginning of the end.

SLIGHTLY
Mrs. Darling was a lovely lady, with a romantic mind and
such a sweet mocking mouth. Her romantic mind was like
the tiny boxes, one within the other, that come from the
puzzling East. However many you discover there is always
one more. Her sweet mocking mouth had one kiss on it that
Wendy could never get, though there it was, perfectly
conspicuous in the right-hand corner.

WENDY
Wendy came first.

JOHN
Then John.

MRS. DARLING
Then Michael.

> *(Mrs. Darling holds baby Michael in her arms.)*

NIBS
There never was a simpler happier family until the coming
of Peter Pan.

> *(The family poses for a picture. Sound of a flash.
> Baby Michael dies in Mrs. Darling's arms.)*

2. MICHAEL

> *(A clock strikes. It starts to rain. The sounds of
> birds and babies. Mrs. Darling, John and Wendy
> stand outside under umbrellas. During the
> following, Wendy and John take baby Michael
> from Mrs. Darling. They put him into the ground
> and bury him under the nursery floorboards.)*

TOOTLES

I don't know whether you have ever seen a map of a child's mind. It is not only confused, but keeps going round all the time. There are zigzag lines on it, just like your temperature on a card, and these are probably roads in the island, for the Neverland is always more or less an island, with astonishing splashes of color here and there. And coral reefs, and rakish-looking craft in the offing.

NIBS

And savages in lonely lairs.

SLIGHTLY

And gnomes who are mostly tailors.

NIBS

And caves through which a river runs.

TOOTLES

And princes with six elder brothers.

SLIGHTLY

And a hut fast going to decay.

NIBS

And one very small old lady with a hooked nose.

TOOTLES

It would be an easy map if that were all, but there is also:

SLIGHTLY

First day at school.

NIBS

Religion.

TOOTLES

Fathers.

SLIGHTLY

The round pond.

NIBS

Needle-work.

TOOTLES

Murders.

NIBS

Hangings.

SLIGHTLY

Verbs that take the dative.

TOOTLES

Chocolate-pudding day.

NIBS

Getting into braces.

SLIGHTLY

Say ninety-nine.

TOOTLES

Three-pence for pulling out your tooth yourself, and so forth. It is all part of the map, and it is all rather confusing, especially as nothing will stand still. The Neverland is made up of dreams…

(Wendy and John open the nursery window. Stars. They exit through the door.)

And of course the Neverlands vary a good deal. On these magic shores children at play are forever beaching their coracles. We too have been there. We can still hear the sound of the surf, though we shall land there no more.

(Tootles exits. The nursery. Months later. Mrs. Darling lies on Wendy's bed in the dark. Sound of a clock ticking. Wendy and John appear at the door.)

JOHN

Mother?...   Mother?...

MRS. DARLING

Michael?

JOHN

No. No, Mother, it's John.

WENDY

You must eat something, Mother. You must take your medicine. You promised you would.

(Wendy pours the medicine into a spoon and gives it to her mother. Mrs. Darling refuses, throws the spoon on the floor. She stares out the window.)

Michael's not here, Mother. He's gone.

MRS. DARLING

Shhhh. I saw. I swear, I saw a face at the window.

JOHN

A face at the window? It's three floors up, Mother.

MRS. DARLING

It was a boy. A little boy. I saw his shadow.

JOHN

Shadow?

MRS. DARLING

A shadow of a boy. It, it wanted me to jump out the window.
So I caught it. I rolled it up and I shut it up in that drawer.

WENDY

Please take your medicine, Mother. You promised you
would.

(Wendy feeds Mrs. Darling the medicine.)

MRS. DARLING

Wendy, you're so grown up. I'm so sorry. ...Enough of this.
To bed with you both.

WENDY

Will you be all right, Mother?

MRS. DARLING

Of course, Wendy. We shall all be all right.

JOHN

You can sleep in here with us again tonight Mother.

MRS. DARLING

No, John. I shall be fine.

JOHN

Mother, you know I get scared when it gets dark as well.

MRS. DARLING

That's why we have the nightlights.

(She lights the nightlights and puts them to bed.)

JOHN

Tell us a story.

WENDY

Yes, a story. Like before.

JOHN

Like you used to.

MRS. DARLING

I don't know a story to tell.

JOHN

Tell about the stars. Michael used to like to hear that one.

MRS. DARLING

You're right John. Michael did like to hear that one.

(Mrs. Darling looks out the window.)

Stars are beautiful, but they may not take an active part in anything. They must just look on forever. It is a punishment put on them for something they did so long ago that no star now even knows what it was. So the older ones have become glassy-eyed and seldom speak – they only wink – which is the star language... *(She's forgotten the story.)*

WENDY

But the little ones...

MRS. DARLING

...But the little ones, they still wonder. And if you listen very closely, the smallest of all the stars in the Milky Way may talk to you.

JOHN/WENDY

And what would they say Mother?

MRS. DARLING

They would say: "Go to sleep children and have the sweetest of dreams." Now say your prayers.

(John and Wendy kneel at their beds. During the following, Mrs. Darling goes to the window and stands up on the ledge.)

JOHN/WENDY

Now I lay me down to sleep,
I pray the Lord my soul to keep,
If I shall die before I wake,
I pray the Lord my soul to take.

(John sees Mrs. Darling standing on the window ledge.)

JOHN

Mother!

(Wendy and John get Mrs. Darling down from the ledge.)

MRS. DARLING

I just wanted to see the stars.

JOHN

Please, Mother, I'm so frightened.

WENDY

Put us to bed Mother.

MRS. DARLING

To bed? To bed.

WENDY

Nothing can harm us, mother, can it? After the nightlights are lit?

MRS. DARLING

What? ...Nothing precious. They are the eyes a mother leaves behind her to guard her children.

WENDY

Goodnight Mother.

JOHN

Goodnight Mother.

MRS. DARLING

Goodnight children. Dear nightlights that protect my
sleeping babes, burn clear and steadfast tonight.

*(Mrs. Darling exits. The children fall asleep. A
strange darkness creeps over the nursery.)*

3. COME AWAY, COME AWAY

OFF STAGE VOICES

(Whispering.) Come away... Come away... Come away...

*(The window opens and a gust of wind comes
into the room. The nightlights flicker and blow
out. Peter Pan flies in through the window.)*

PETER

Tinker Bell? Tink, where are you?

(Michael's crib lights up.)

Come out of there Do you know where they put my shadow?
Show me.

*(Tinker Bell – who we only see as light - shows
Peter the chest of drawers. Peter opens a drawer
and his shadow flies out. Tinker Bell gets shut in
the drawer. Peter chases his shadow, catches it,*

*and fights with it. He wrestles it to the floor and
tries to reattach it to himself. He can't do it. In
his frustration he starts crying on the floor.
Wendy wakes and sits up in bed.)*

WENDY

Michael? ...Boy, why are you crying?

PETER

What's your name?

WENDY

Wendy Moira Angela Darling. What's yours?

PETER

Peter Pan.

WENDY

Is that all?

PETER

Yes.

WENDY

I'm so sorry. Is, is this a dream?

PETER

No.

WENDY

How do you know?

PETER

I know.

WENDY

Where do you come from?

PETER
Second to the right, and then straight on till morning.

WENDY
What a funny address.

PETER
No, it's not.

WENDY
I mean, is that what they put on the letters?

PETER
Don't get any letters.

WENDY
But your mother gets letters?

PETER
What?

WENDY
Your mother-

PETER
I don't have a mother.

WENDY
Oh Peter, no wonder you were crying.

PETER
I wasn't crying about my mother. I hate mothers. I was
crying because I can't get my shadow to stick on.

WENDY
It's come off? How awful!

PETER

I keep losing it. It hates me. It keeps running away and doing the most fantastic things without me.

WENDY

I think your shadow came to my mother.

PETER

It did? What did it do?

WENDY

It tried to get her to jump out the window.

(Peter finds this very funny.)

PETER

I can't get it to stick back on.

WENDY

Peter, It could be sewn on.

PETER

What is "sewn"?

WENDY

You're dreadfully ignorant.

PETER

No, I'm not.

WENDY

I shall sew it on for you, my little man.

(Wendy gets a needle and thread.)

Stay still. I dare say it will hurt a little.

PETER

I won't cry. I never do.

(Wendy sews Peter's shadow onto him.)

WENDY

All finished.

PETER

My shadow is dead. You killed it.

WENDY

No, it isn't dead. It just needs some light.

(She lights a lamp. The shadow wakes up. Peter and his shadow play together. He crows.)

PETER

Look, it's alive. I got it back. Wendy, look, look! How clever I am! Oh, the cleverness of me!

WENDY

You're conceited. Of course, I did nothing!

PETER

You did a little.

WENDY

A little? Goodnight.

(Wendy gets back into her bed and covers her face with the blanket.)

PETER

Wendy. Wendy, don't go back to sleep, there's so much to do. Don't waste time dreaming while I'm here.

(He goes to her bed.)

PETER (CONT)
Wendy, I can't help crowing when I'm pleased with myself.
Wendy... Wendy, one girl is better than twenty boys.

WENDY
Do you really think so, Peter?

PETER
Yes, I do.

WENDY
Really?

PETER
Yes.

WENDY
I think it's perfectly sweet of you. I shall give you a kiss if
you like.

PETER
Thank you. *(Holds out his hand.)*

WENDY
Don't you know what a kiss is?

PETER
I'll know when you give it to me.

>   *(Not to hurt his feelings, she gives him her
>   thimble.)*

Now shall I give you a kiss?

WENDY

If you please.

*(She prepares for a kiss. He pulls an acorn
button out and gives it to her.)*

Oh. I will wear it on this chain around my neck. ...Peter, how
old are you?

PETER

Don't know. Quite young I guess. I ran away the day I was
born.

WENDY

You ran away, why?

PETER

Because I heard mother talking about what I was to be when
I became a man. She picked me up, and held me in her arms
and she said "One day, you will be a man, my little man. And
you shall make me so happy." Grownups don't think
children can understand what they say - but we do. I don't
want to be a man. I want to always be a little boy and to have
fun. I hate grownups. So I ran away to Kensington Gardens
and lived a long, long time with the fairies.

WENDY

You know fairies, Peter?

PETER

Yes. I used to know millions of them, but they're almost all
dead now. You see, Wendy, when the first baby laughed for
the first time, that laugh broke into a thousand pieces, and
they all went skipping about, and that was the beginning of
fairies. And now, whenever a new baby is born its first laugh
becomes a fairy. So there ought to be one fairy for every boy
and girl.

WENDY

Ought to be? Isn't there?

PETER

No. Children grow up so fast now. Some of them don't believe in fairies, and every time a child says: "I don't believe in fairies" there's a fairy somewhere that falls down dead. They just crumple up.

WENDY

But you just said it. You just said: "I don't believe in" –

(Peter covers her mouth.)

PETER

Shhhhhh. I can say it. You can't. ...Tinker Bell? Are you dead? She didn't say it. Where is she? Tink, where are you?

WENDY

Peter, you don't mean to tell me that there is a fairy in this very room?

PETER

She came with me. Do you hear her?

WENDY

(Listens.) I hear... The only sound I hear is like a little tinkle of bells.

PETER

That's her. It's the fairy language.

WENDY

I believe it's coming from over there. *(Indicates chest of drawers.)*

(Peter releases Tinker Bell from the drawer.)

PETER

Well, I'm very sorry, but how could I know you were in there?

WENDY

Oh Peter, if only she would stand still and let me see her!

PETER

Let me catch her.

(He grabs Tinker Bell and shows her to Wendy.)

WENDY

I don't see anything.

PETER

Look closer. You have to try to see her. Try harder. Close your eyes.

(Wendy closes her eyes.)

Picture her. ...Now open them.

(She opens them.)

WENDY

Oh, I see her now. She's lovely! She's the most wonderful thing I've ever seen.

PETER

Tink, I think this lady wishes you were her fairy.

WENDY

What does she say, Peter?

PETER

She says you're an ugly girl, and that she's my fairy. You
know, Tink, you can't be my fairy, because I'm a gentleman
and you are a lady.

(Tinker Bell replies.)

WENDY

What did she say?

PETER

She said "You silly ass." She's not very polite.

WENDY

Peter, where do you live?

PETER

With the lost boys.

WENDY

Lost boys?

PETER

Yes.

WENDY

Who are they?

PETER

They're the ones I steal when their mothers are looking the
other way.

WENDY

What? Where do you find them?

PETER

All over. Some of them I take. Some of them run away, and
they come to me. Some of them fall out of their prams while
their nurses are busy doing something awful. I catch them
and take them to the Neverland.

WENDY

Neverland?

PETER

The island where we live. There are pirates and Indians and
beasts. Boys rule the island. And every time you take a
breath in Neverland, a grown up dies. So I try to take as
many breaths as possible!

WENDY

My, you are a nasty little thing, aren't you?

PETER

There's only one rule there. You can never grow up.
Whenever any of the lost boys seem to be growing up, I thin
them out. Squash them like bugs.

WENDY

Oh my.

PETER

But... Sometimes it's rather lonely. You see we have no
female companionship.

WENDY

Are none of the lost boys girls?

PETER

Oh, no. Girls don't want to be stolen, they don't run away,
and they're much too clever to fall out of their prams.

WENDY

I think it's perfectly lovely the way you talk about girls.
Most boys just find us puzzling. John there just despises us.

PETER

This one?

(Peter starts hitting the sleeping John.)

WENDY

No! Stop, stop!

JOHN

(Half asleep.) Mother?

WENDY

No, John.

JOHN

Oh, You're the boy from Mother's dreams. I must be
dreaming.

WENDY

Yes, John, You're only dreaming. Go back to sleep.

JOHN

Oh, Thank goodness it's a good dream.

(John goes back to sleep.)

WENDY

I know you meant to be kind but you mustn't do that. John's
my brother. You can't just go around hitting people. You
don't know that, do you? It's not your fault you're
completely uncivilized. Well, I still think it was sweet what
you said about girls. I've never met anyone like you, Peter. I
could ask you a hundred questions. You may give me a kiss
if you like

PETER

I thought you would want it back.

WENDY

Oh dear, I don't mean a kiss. I mean a thimble.

PETER

A thimble? What's that?

WENDY

It's like this.

(She goes to kiss him.)

PETER

What are you doing?

WENDY

This.

(She kisses him.)

PETER

Funny. Now shall I give you a thimble?

WENDY

If you wish.

(He kisses her. Beat. Wendy's head jerks back. She screams.)

PETER

What is it, Wendy?

WENDY

Something pulled my hair.

PETER

Tinker Bell! Stop it! I've never seen her be so bad before.

WENDY

She's very impertinent. Peter, why did you really come to our nursery window?

PETER

To try to hear the stories. None of us knows any stories.

WENDY

How perfectly awful.

PETER

Do you know why swallows build in the eaves of houses? To listen to the stories. Wendy, you were telling that boy such a lovely story. I heard you.

WENDY

Which story was it?

PETER

About the prince, who couldn't find the lady who wore the glass slipper.

WENDY

Peter, that was Cinderella.

PETER

What happened? Did he find her?

WENDY

Yes, he found her, and they lived happily ever after.

(Peter hurries to the window.)

WENDY

Where are you going?

                              PETER

To tell the lost boys.

                              WENDY

Don't go, Peter. I know lots of stories. Oh, the stories I could
tell the boys!

              *(Peter wants to rip those stories out of her. He's
              dangerous now.)*

                              PETER

What? Wendy, come with me.

                              WENDY

What?

                              PETER

We'll fly.

                              WENDY

Fly? You can fly?

                              PETER

Yes.

                              WENDY

Oh dear, I can't. No, think of Mother.

                              PETER

Come with me Wendy.

              (He grabs her and pulls her to the window.)

                              WENDY

Let me go! I can't fly.

                              PETER

I'll teach you.

24

WENDY

To fly?

PETER

You want to know a secret? All babies were birds before they were human.

WENDY

What?

PETER

Don't you remember? You were a bird. *(Indicating John.)* He was a bird. Think back. You were wild the first few days of life, and itchy at the shoulders. That's where your wings used to be. I'll teach you to be a bird again, Wendy.

WENDY

What?

PETER

I'll teach you how to jump on the wind's back, and then away we go. We'll soar high above the clouds and sail down low, right on top of the ocean waves, so close that you can touch a shark's tail. Wendy, all the little stars want you to fly with me tonight. Listen, the smallest stars are calling out "Wendy... Wendy... Come away... Come away..." How can you think about sleeping in your stupid bed when you might be flying in the sky with me playing games with those stars? And, Wendy, there are mermaids.

WENDY

Mermaids! With tails?

PETER

Such long tails.

WENDY

Oh, I've always dreamed of seeing a mermaid. But, my mother. She needs me now.

PETER

We need you Wendy. You could be our mother. You could tuck us in at night. None of us has ever been tucked in at night.

WENDY

Oh.

PETER

And you could make pockets for us. You could take care of us all. And you could pretend anything you want and it will be real, Wendy. We can play make believe forever and ever. I'll show you things you can't even see in your dreams.

WENDY

Oh, Peter. Would you teach John to fly too?

PETER

If you like.

WENDY

John, wake up, wake up.

JOHN

Is this still a dream?

WENDY

No John, this is not a dream. This is very real.

JOHN

Then I shall wake up. I am up. Oh my. The strange boy from my dream is still here, isn't he?

WENDY

This boy has come to teach us to fly.

JOHN

To fly? I say, can you really fly?

PETER

Watch this..

(Peter flies around the room.)

JOHN

That's absolutely ridiculous!

WENDY

How sweet!

PETER

Yes, I'm sweet. Oh, I'm sweet!

JOHN

How do you do it?

PETER

You just think wonderful thoughts and they lift you up in the air.

(He is off again.)

JOHN

Wonderful thoughts? Wendy, I don't have many of those.

WENDY

Try, John. Try.

(They try to think wonderful thoughts and fly. It doesn't work.)

JOHN

It doesn't work. I keep thinking of Michael and Mother.

WENDY

Think back before that John. Before everything. *(They try
again.)* Think back to good dreams, to playing games, and
telling secrets, and eating chocolate, and flying off our beds.

JOHN

I'm trying. I've got it now, Wendy.

> *(John jumps off the bed and falls flat on his
> face.)*

No. I just go down instead of up.

PETER

I must blow the fairy dust on you first.

> *(He blows some fairy dust on John and Wendy.)*

Now try. Just wiggle your shoulders this way, like a bird.
Think wonderful thoughts. And up you go.

> *(John and Wendy try it and they fly.)*

WENDY

Oh, lovely!

JOHN

Look at me! Look at me! How ripping!

PETER

Shall we see the mermaids, Wendy?

WENDY

Mermaids!

PETER

And the pirates?

JOHN

Pirates!

PETER

We'll fly like birds again! Come away!

> *(John grabs his Sunday hat. Peter crows. The
> children fly out of the nursery, into the night
> sky.)*

4. THE FLIGHT

> *(The nursery transforms into the night sky.
> Wind. Stars. Peter, Wendy and John fly up, down
> and all around. Time passes.)*

WENDY

How many seas have we passed, John? How many moons?
How many nights have we been flying?

JOHN

I've lost track, Wendy. I can't remember.

PETER

Follow me!

> *(Peter does tricks in the air. Time passes. They
> fly.)*

JOHN

Here's a funny thought. Flying is rather lonely. You wouldn't
think it. But even when you're flying with other people,
you're always flying by yourself.

(Time passes. They fly.)

PETER

You. Who are you?

WENDY

I'm Wendy.

JOHN

And I'm John.

PETER

Oh, Wendy, Yes, yes. We're getting close. If you ever find me forgetting you, just keep on saying: "I'm Wendy, I'm Wendy" and then I'll remember.

JOHN

(To Wendy.) That's rather worrisome.

PETER

There it is.

WENDY

Where, where?

PETER

There! Where all the golden arrows are pointing. The Neverland. Would you like an adventure now, or tea first?

JOHN

Tea first!

PETER

To the Neverland!

(They fly away.)

5. THE ISLAND COME TRUE

*(Hands poke through holes in the nursery wall.
They beckon us to come to the island.)*

SLIGHTLY/NIBS/TOOTLES
(Whispering.) Come away... Come away... Come away...

*(During the following, the nursery transforms.
Mist fills the space. The nursery starts to
vegetate. Leaves fall from the sky. Trees, and
vines grow out of the ground. It's the Neverland
but it's also always the nursery at the same time.
The two worlds exist as one. The nursery keeps
transforming, changing, growing as the play
goes along. It never stays the same.)*

SLIGHTLY
Of all delectable islands the Neverland is the snuggest and
most compact, not large and sprawly, you know, with tedious
distances between one adventure and another, but nicely
crammed.

NIBS
Feeling that Peter was on his way back, the Neverland had
again woke into life. If you put your ear to the ground, you
would hear the whole island seething with life.

TOOTLES
When you play at it by day with the chairs and tablecloth, it
is not in the least alarming, but in the two minutes before
you go to sleep it becomes very real.

*(Slightly throws a pile of leaves in the air. The
lost boys begin their circle game.)*

SLIGHTLY
The lost boys were out looking for Peter.

(Walking in a circle, the children become lost boys.)

TOOTLES

The pirates were out looking for the lost boys.

(Walking in a circle, the lost boys become pirates.)

NIBS

The Indians were out looking for the pirates.

(Walking in a circle, the pirates become Indians.)

SLIGHTLY

And the beasts were out looking for the Indians.

(Walking in a circle, the Indians become beasts.)

NIBS

They were going round and round the island, but they didn't meet because they were all going at the same rate.

SLIGHTLY

All wanted blood

TOOTLES

Except the boys,

NIBS

Who liked it by rule,

SLIGHTLY

But tonight were out to

SLIGHTLY/TOOTLES/NIBS

Greet their captain.

6. THE LOST BOYS

(The lost boys sit and wait for Peter to come back – like dogs waiting for the master to tell them that the day has begun.)

TOOTLES

Where is Peter? Has he come back yet, Slightly?

SLIGHTLY

No, Tootles, no.

TOOTLES

I do wish he would come back. I'm suffering from severe depression.

NIBS

What is depression, Tootles?

TOOTLES

I'm not quite sure. But I think it's when you miss something so badly, but you don't quite know what it is you're missing.

NIBS

You miss Peter.

TOOTLES

Yes, but I miss something else too. Something much bigger than Peter. Oh, I'm incredibly anxious when he's away. I'm so afraid the pirates will murder us if he's not here to protect us.

SLIGHTLY

Don't be afraid of the smelly old pirates. I'll protect you, Tootles. Nothing frightens me. Not no bloody pirates.

NIBS

I just wish Peter would come back and tell us whether he has heard anything more about Cinderella. Slightly, I dreamt last night that the prince found Cinderella and he gave her the slipper and she gave him a blue snake. I drew a picture of it. It was a splendid dream.

TOOTLES

I am awfully anxious about Cinderella as well. I do hope Peter has heard what's become of her. Did the prince find her? I hope so. Was she slaughtered by pirates? I hope not. I'm awfully fond of her. You see, not knowing anything about my own mother I am fond of thinking that she was rather like Cinderella.

SLIGHTLY

You know Peter has forbidden us to speak about our mothers.

NIBS

All I remember about my mother is that she often said to my father, "Oh, how I wish I had a check book of my own." I don't know what a check book is, but if I ever found one, I should just love to give my mother one.

SLIGHTLY

My mother was fonder of me than your mothers were of you.

NIBS

No she wasn't!

TOOTLES

No!

SLIGHTLY

Oh yes, she was. Peter had to make up names for all of you, but my mother had written on the pinafore I was lost in. "Slightly soiled." That's my name.

*(The lost boys wrestle. Sounds and shadows in
the woods.)*

LOST BOYS

Pirates!

*(The lost boys run. They put on costume pieces
in front of us – an eye patch, beard, etc. and
become the pirates. Slightly becomes Starkey,
Nibs becomes Bill Jukes and Tootles becomes
Smee.)*

<u>7. HOOK</u>

STARKEY/BILL JUKES/SMEE (CHANT.)

When he smells blood, then he appears.
The cruelest in the book.
They'll be nothing left but children's bones,
Once you've shaken claws with Hook!

*(A shadow appears behind the nursery wall – we
see a hook first - and then the rest of his shadow.
Hook rips a hole in the nursery wallpaper with
his hook and climbs through. He sniffs the air.
He's a man on the hunt.)*

HOOK

I smell boy...

There were children here. The filthy rats must have just
scuttled away. How do they always disappear? I want them
dead!

PIRATES

Ay, ay.

BILL JUKES

(Getting out his pistol.) I'll after 'em. I'll shoot 'em, dead,
Captain.

HOOK

Ay, and the sound will bring Tiger Lily's pack upon us. Do
you want to lose your scalp?

BILL JUKES

No, Captain.

HOOK

Idiot! Your voices frightened them away! How many times
must I tell you scags? When you kill, you must kill silently.

BILL JUKES

Silently?

HOOK

Yes, silently. Like this.

> *(Hook slits Bill Jukes throat silently in one
> motion with his hook. Bill Jukes falls to the floor
> and dies.)*

...Oh, what a mess.

SMEE

Very effective, Captain.

STARKEY

I'll mischief those boys, Captain, and tickle them with
Johnny Corkscrew. Johnny's a silent fellow.

HOOK

Scatter and look for them! I want boy blood!

(Starkey drags off Bill Jukes' dead body and exits. Hook and Smee alone.)

HOOK

Oh, my head aches, Smee. How I hate children. They're an affront to my senses. They make my eyes water. Their scent molests my nose hairs. Their monstrous little voices are miniature swords piercing at my temples. I want to kill them all.

SMEE

I know Captain.

HOOK

Most of all, I want that boy. You know of whom I speak. The insect that makes my hook twitch. Oh, I'll break him into a hundred little pieces. Tear off his flesh limb from limb. I want his blood. I want to split him open, shred him, gnaw at his boy bones. I shall make him rue the day he cut off my arm.

SMEE

And yet, I have often heard you say that hook was worth a score of hands. At least when it comes to the combing of hair, and the slaughter of children.

HOOK

Ay, if I was a mother, Smee, I would pray to have my babes born with this *(indicates hook.)* instead of that. *(indicates hand.)* All children should know such suffering. That maggot just flung my arm to that crocodile like a piece of raw meat. I'm not raw meat, Smee!

SMEE

No, no, no you're not, are you Captain, I know, I know.

HOOK

The crocodile liked my arm so much, Smee, that he has
followed me ever since, from sea to sea and from land to
land, licking his beastly lips for the rest of me.

SMEE

In a way it is a sort of compliment.

HOOK

I want no such compliments. I want that boy who first gave
the creature his taste for me. Thank the stars the monster
swallowed that clock. You know something, Smee? That
clock has saved my life. It lives deep inside the creature and
it goes tick, tick, tick, tick, tick, tick, tick, tick, tick, inside
him… as if to warn me every time he's coming for me.

SMEE

Some day that clock will run down though, and then that
croc, he'll get you, won't he?

HOOK

Why would you say that to me, Smee, when you know that's
the fear that haunts me? Oh, I'm so sick of this endless
game. What has that infant done to me? The crocodile haunts
my days and that boy haunts my dreams. *(A
confession.)* ...Smee, his shadow visits me at night.

SMEE

His shadow?

HOOK

Ay, his shadow.

SMEE

The crocodile's?

HOOK

Pan's shadow! ...It comes to me at night and does the strangest things to me.

SMEE

What does it do?

HOOK

It taunts me. Teases me. ...Strangles me.

SMEE

Strangles you?

HOOK

Ay, strangles me in my sleep. ...Sometimes, in my dream, Pan is riding that crocodile towards me with that smug little smile on his grubby face and the clock inside the croc has run out. Sometimes I fear I'll go deaf, and the monster will swallow me whole. And sometimes... And this might be the fear that haunts me the most. I fear the only sound that I'll ever hear as long as I'm awake - until the end of my days – until my final breath - is that endless ticking... until I die... Tick, tick, tick...Tick, tick, tick... Do you hear that, Smee? ...Do you hear that?

SMEE

What? What? What?

HOOK

Children.

> *(Hook follows his ear to the ground and reveals a trap in the floor. Hook and Smee open it. Smoke comes out. The sound of children's voices from below.)*

Odds, bobs, hammer, and tongs.

SMEE

A chimney!

HOOK

Listen, Smee. The children. They live beneath the ground!

SMEE

I hear the little buggers. Do you hear them say Peter Pan's away from home?

HOOK

He'll be back with more bloody children. *(Whispers into the hole.)* Little boy, little boy, I'm coming for you...

(He closes the trap.)

I'll bide my time, and when Pan returns I'll crush him. I'll skewer him from eyeball to elbow. I'll eat him alive. I'll kill them all. Ahahaha, There is nothing more festive than dead children!

(Hook laughs. Sound of a ticking clock. A shadow lurks.)

HOOK

What's that sound?

SMEE

I don't hear anything.

HOOK

You don't hear that? The clock. The clock. The crocodile! The crocodile!

(The crocodile's shadow appears and chases Hook and Smee away.)

8. THE WHITE BIRD

(The Lost Boys pop up from under the ground.)

SLIGHTLY

The Pirates are gone. All clear.

TOOTLES

Oh, I do wish Peter was here. I'm so afraid the pirates will
eat me.

*(Nibs sees something in the sky. It's Wendy flying
above.)*

NIBS

Lads! Lads!

SLIGHTLY

What is it, Nibs?

WENDY

(Flying above.) Poor Wendy!

NIBS

A great white bird! It is flying this way!

TOOTLES

What kind of a bird, do you think?

NIBS

I don't know, I've never seen anything like it. But it looks so
weary, and as it flies it moans "Poor Wendy."

TOOTLES

Poor Wendy?

SLIGHTLY

I remember now there are birds called Wendies.

(It begins to snow.)

NIBS

See, it comes, The Wendy! How white it is! Look. The snow
is coming with it.

TOOTLES

Perhaps it is the mother of snow.

SLIGHTLY

You're always thinking of mothers.

(Tinker Bell flies in.)

NIBS

Tinker Bell. Hello, Tink! *(Tink responds.)* What? She says
Peter wants us to shoot the Wendy.

TOOTLES

Let us do what Peter wishes!

SLIGHTLY

Ay, shoot it. Quick, bows and arrows!

TOOTLES

Out of the way, Tink. I'll shoot it.

> *(Tootles shoots Wendy with an arrow. She falls to
> the ground.)*

I have shot the Wendy. Peter will be so pleased.

> *(The boys gather around Wendy and examine
> her.)*

TOOTLES (Cont)

I shot the Wendy Bird! I shot the Wendy Bird! I shot the
Wendy Bird! I shot the Wendy Bird!

SLIGHTLY

That is no bird. That is a lady.

TOOTLES

A lady?

SLIGHTLY

And Tootles has killed her.

NIBS

Now I see, Peter was bringing her to us. A mother. To take
care of us. Oh, Tootles.

*(Tootles goes to Wendy and kneels. He realizes
what he has done.)*

TOOTLES

I did it. I killed her. I killed Cinderella. When the lady used
to come to me in my dreams, I said, "Pretty mother, pretty
mother," and I would kiss her. But when at last she really
came, I murdered her. May my mother never come to me
again, not even in my dreams, for she has my arrow in her
heart. Friends, goodbye.

(Tootles starts to go.)

NIBS

Don't go.

TOOTLES

I must. I'm so afraid of Peter.

(Sound of Peter crowing.)

ALL

Peter!

SLIGHTLY

Hide her!

> *(The boys hide the dead Wendy under a pile of leaves and stand in front of her. Peter flies in.)*

PETER

Greetings, boys! I'm back. Why do you not cheer? *(They cheer.)* Great news, boys, I have brought a mother for all of you at last.

SLIGHTLY

Ay, ay.

PETER

Have you not seen her? She flew this way.

TOOTLES

Peter, I will show her to you.

SLIGHTLY/NIBS

No, no.

TOOTLES

Stand back all, and let Peter see.

> *(The boys stand back and reveal Wendy on the ground.)*

PETER

Wendy, with an arrow in her heart. She's dead.

NIBS

I thought it was only flowers that died.

PETER

Whose arrow?

TOOTLES

Mine, Peter. I killed her. I killed the mother. Strike, Peter.
Strike true.

(Peter moves to attack Tootles with the arrow.)

SLIGHTLY

The Wendy Lady, she's moving!

(Slightly and Nibs go to Wendy.)

NIBS

She lives!

SLIGHTLY

The Wendy lady lives.

*(Peter stops and goes to Wendy. He holds up the
button she has attached to her chain.)*

PETER

Look, the arrow struck against this. It's the kiss I gave her. It
saved her life.

SLIGHTLY

I remember kisses. Kisses are wonderful things. Let me see
it. Ay, that is a kiss.

PETER

Wendy, get better quickly and I'll take you to see the
mermaids. She really wanted to see a mermaid.

NIBS

Tinker Bell. She said to shoot the Wendy.

PETER

She said that? Tinker Bell. You told them to kill Wendy?
Tinker Bell, I am your friend no more.

NIBS

She's crying. She says she is your fairy.

PETER

You're not my fairy. Begone.

(Tinker Bell flies away.)

Now... what shall we do with Wendy?

NIBS

We should carry her down into the house.

SLIGHTLY

Ay, that is what one does with ladies.

PETER

No, don't touch her.

SLIGHTLY

That's what I was thinking.

PETER

We can't move her. She has to get better.

NIBS

But if she lies there she will die.

SLIGHTLY

Ay, she will die. It's a pity, but there is no way out.

PETER

Let us build a little house around her.

9. THE LITTLE HOUSE

(John appears flying in the sky.)

NIBS

What is that?

(John falls from the sky.)

JOHN

Ahhhhhhhh!

(He lands on the ground.)

This is absolutely the most horrible dream I've ever had. Wake up John. *(He smacks himself.)* Wake up. *(He smacks himself again.)* Wake up.

PETER

Who are you?

JOHN

Why must you always forget me? I'm John. Wendy's brother. Now where is Wendy?

PETER

There. She's asleep. Nibs, Tootles, see that this boy helps build the house.

NIBS

Ay, ay, sir.

JOHN

Build a house?

NIBS

For the Wendy.

JOHN

The Wendy? *My* Wendy? Why, she is only a girl.

NIBS

That is why we are her servants.

JOHN

You? Wendy's servants!

PETER

Yes, and so are you! Now, let's build Wendy a house.

> *(Music. The lost boys empty their pockets and build the house around Wendy out of the most humble and absurd materials – string, broken toys, leaves, balls, etc. – objects from children's pockets and all the furniture from the nursery. They run back and forth with various objects. Finally, the little house is built around Wendy. Fours walls, a roof and a door.)*

PETER

There's no knocker on the door.

> *(Tootles gives the sole of his shoe and it makes an excellent knocker.)*

SLIGHTLY

There's no chimney.

> *(Peter takes John's hat and places it on the roof. The Lost Boys wait outside the house for Wendy. Peter knocks on the door, and after a moment of suspense, Wendy comes out.)*

WENDY

(Shocked.) Good night.

SLIGHTLY

Wendy lady, for you we built this house.

NIBS

Oh, say you're pleased.

WENDY

Lovely, darling little house.

TOOTLES

And we are your children.

LOST BOYS

Wendy lady, please be our mother.

WENDY

Ought I? Of course it's frightfully fascinating, but you see I'm only a little girl. I have no real experience.

SLIGHTLY

That doesn't matter. What we need is just a nice motherly person.

WENDY

Oh dear! You see, I feel that's exactly what I am.

TOOTLES

It is, it is.

SLIGHTLY

I saw it at once.

WENDY

Very well then, I will do my best. Come inside at once, you naughty children. And before I put you to bed I will finish the story of Cinderella.

*(They all squeeze into the little house they have
built. The little house lights up from inside. Peter
stands guard outside. Night. Stars. Peter falls
asleep outside the house. Maybe the house floats
up to the sky like a magic trick. Maybe the
children take the house apart bit by bit.)*

10. THE MERMAID'S LAGOON

*(During the following, the children create the
Mermaid's lagoon around the nursery dresser,
which becomes Marooner's Rock.)*

NIBS

If you shut your eyes and are a lucky one, you may see at
times a shapeless pool of lovely pale colors suspended in the
darkness. Then if you squeeze your eyes tighter, the pool
begins to take shape, and the colors become so vivid that
with another squeeze they must go on fire. But just before
they go on fire you see the Mermaid's Lagoon.

WENDY

Oh, I wish I were a mermaid. I wish I had a long tail and I
could breath under water. Neverland makes me feel as if I'm
under water all the time. I feel my body changing, every
minute. As if something's racing inside of me, like a clock
ticking. Or a tea kettle. I get hot and then cold again so
easily. My skin feels like it's on fire. It's like water moving
inside of me, rippling inside of me, all the time. I can't get
my balance. I can't catch my breath. It's scary and wonderful
all at the same time.

*(Peter and Wendy are sitting on the rock,
dipping their feet in the imaginary water. Night.)*

WENDY (Cont)

I love making ripples in the water, don't you? Look at our reflections in the water. There's you and there's me. Peter, do you know the difference between girls and boys?

PETER

Girls are softer than boys.

WENDY

Your skin is very soft. Oh, your face is so young. You're like a grown baby.

PETER

I'm not a baby.

WENDY

You still have your first teeth. But, your eyes are old. …You look like Michael. He was only a baby, but his eyes were old too. …For so long I waited for a change. When Michael died everything changed, but I'm not sure how much I have. You can see it in Mother's face and I wonder if you can see it in mine. …What do you remember about your mother, Peter?

PETER

Nothing.

WENDY

I want to be a mother. I want to have a baby.

PETER

You can't grow up here, Wendy. That's the only rule.

WENDY

I know.

PETER

Wendy, don't change. Don't get old. Promise me, you'll
never grow up. Because growing up is like dying. No matter
what happens. Just promise me.

WENDY

I promise.

PETER

Whatever you want, Wendy, we can just pretend, All right?

WENDY

Will you pretend to be Father, Peter?

PETER

If you wish it.

WENDY

And we can pretend the lost boys are our children?

PETER

Yes, but only pretend.

WENDY

Yes, I know, of course. But it is what I wish. Have you ever
been in love Peter?

PETER

What is it?

WENDY

Oh Peter, you don't know what love is?

PETER

Is it a place?

WENDY

Yes, I imagine it is. It's like being taken from somewhere you've known all your life to a new place you don't know anything about. Somewhere you've only dreamed of.

Everything smells different. Everything feels new. And you feel new. Your skin feels new. Like a baby.

(She touches his chest.)

Peter, your heart is beating like a drum. Like a real boy.

(She kisses him. – Suddenly, a scream is heard. Drums. Smee and Starkey are seen in the gloom rowing a little boat. They have the Indian princess Tiger Lily tied up.)

11. MAROONER'S ROCK

(Peter and Wendy jump off the rock and hide in the water.)

SMEE

(To Tiger Lily.) Silence! *(To Starkey.)* Luff, you lubber, luff!

WENDY

Tiger Lily!

STARKEY

What was that?

(Peter and Wendy bob in the water.)

SMEE

Must be one of them mermaids. Careful Starkey, them mermaids are pretty but dodgy creatures. I wouldn't trust 'em further than I can spit.

> *(Smee and Starkey tie up Tiger Lily on the rock.)*

Now you die, savage.

> *(During the following, Peter is hidden from Smee and Starkey. They only hear his voice.)*

PETER

(Imitating Hook.) Ahoy there, you scags!

SMEE

The captain!

STARKEY

From the water.

SMEE

We have put the girl on the rock, Captain.

PETER

(Imitating Hook.) Set her free.

SMEE

Free?

PETER

(Imitating Hook.) Yes, cut her bonds and let her go.

STARKEY

Do you want us to slit her throat instead?

PETER

(Imitating Hook.) Set her free.

                          SMEE

But, captain -

                          PETER

(Imitating Hook.) At once, d'ye hear, or I'll plunge my hook
in you.

                        STARKEY

This is queer!

                          SMEE

Better do what the captain orders.

                        STARKEY

Ay, ay.

          *(He cuts Tiger Lily's cords. She slips into the
          water and swims away.)*

                          HOOK

Boat ahoy!

          *(The real Hook appears. Starkey and Smee pick
          him up in the boat.)*

                          SMEE

You look weary, Captain. Is all well?

                          HOOK

The game is up. Those repulsive boys have found themselves
a mother.

          (Peter pulls Wendy beneath the water.)

What was that?

*(The Neverbird – a feather or perhaps an article
of baby Michael's clothing, operated by John,
drifts on the water in her nest, which is
Michael's crib.)*

SMEE

Looks like a Neverbird. ...Speaking of mothers, would you
look at that? It's a nest. It must have fallen into the water, but
would a mother desert her eggs?

HOOK

Shut up, Smee. Get the mother, and you can crack the egg.
That's how to get Pan. We must take away his precious little
mother. We will seize the little maggots, carry them off to the
ship, and kill them all.

*(Hook calls to the Neverbird, pets it, then at
once grabs one of the eggs and cracks it with his
hook. He laughs.)*

Oh, How I love the sight of a Mother watching her baby die.

*(The Neverbird attacks him and Hook throws the
bird back into the water. The Neverbird returns
to her nest to protect her remaining eggs. The
Neverbird cries.)*

Now... where is Tiger Lily?

SMEE

That's all right, Captain. We let her go.

HOOK

You what?

SMEE

We let her go.

HOOK

Let her go?

STARKEY

You called over the water to us to let her go.

HOOK

Brimstone and gall, what cozening is here? I gave no such order.

STARKEY

The voice, in the water. It sounded just like you.

HOOK

Did it?

STARKEY

Ay, it did, Captain. Just like you.

HOOK

Did it now? Did the voice in the water sound something like this? "You stupid dog!"

STARKEY

Right.

HOOK

"You slime! You sea scum! You oily bilge rat!"

STARKEY

A bit like that, yes.

HOOK

"You weaselly, worthless worm! Your flesh shall feed the fish!" Die! Die! Die!

> *(Hook viciously kills Starkey. Blood splatters. Hook throws his body into the lagoon.)*

SMEE

Not another one, Captain

HOOK

Shut up, Smee.

PETER

(Imitating Hook.) Shut up, Smee.

> *(Peter is hiding. Hook can't see him. The lagoon gets darker and darker. Mist rises.)*

HOOK

What was that?

PETER

(Imitating Hook.) What was that?

HOOK

Hello?...

PETER

(Imitating Hook.) Hello?...

HOOK

Spirit that haunts this dark lagoon tonight, do you hear me?

PETER

(Imitating Hook.) Odds, bobs, hammer and tongs, I hear you.

HOOK

Who are you, stranger? Speak.

PETER

(Imitating Hook.) I am James Hook, Captain of the Jolly Roger.

HOOK

(Terrified.) 'Tis my shadow. If you are Hook, come tell me, who am I?

PETER

(Imitating Hook.) A dead man.

HOOK

I'm not dead. You are.

PETER

(Imitating Hook.) Hahahaha.

HOOK

'Tis the devil! ...Shadow, have you another voice?

PETER

I have.

HOOK

And another name?

PETER

Yes.

HOOK

Ghost?

PETER

No.

HOOK

Animal?

PETER

Yes.

                         HOOK

Man?

                         PETER

No!

                         HOOK

Boy?

                         PETER

Yes.

                         HOOK

Ordinary boy?

                         PETER

No.

                         HOOK

Filthy, disgusting, monster of a boy?

                         PETER

No.

                         HOOK

The boy who haunts my dreams?

            (Peter crows. Hook sees him.)

Pan!

            *(Hook cuts Peter with his hook. He hurts him
            badly. Peter is bleeding.)*

Bleed, boy! Bleed!

            *(Hook pushes Peter against the rock and chokes
            him.)*

HOOK (Cont)

A hand doesn't come without a price, boy. An eye for an eye, a tooth for a tooth, a hand for a hand. I'm going to take back what you took from me, boy. Body part by body part. Cut by bloody cut. Which part should I take first? A foot? A head? A hand?

> *(The sound of a ticking clock and shadows appear in the lagoon.)*

That sound... That sound... Is it real? Or just inside my head!?!

SMEE

The clock. The clock. The croc. ...The crocodile! It smells the blood.

> *(The crocodile's shadow circles the rock in the water.)*

HOOK

No, no, no! Save me, Smee. Save me!

> *(Smee and Hook board the boat. Smee paddles away during the following.)*

This isn't over yet, Pan. I'll crush you. I'll stain the water with your blood. I'll pluck out your hairs and make a wig out of 'em! I'll stretch your porcelain skin into my boots. I'll pull out your baby teeth and wear them as a pearl necklace! Bleed! Bleed! Bleed! I'm coming for you, boy!...

> *(Hook's boat disappears. Wendy appears and pulls Peter up onto the rock and they lay down beside each other. The water is rising. They will soon be drowned.)*

WENDY

Peter!

PETER

Wendy, the rock is getting smaller. The tide. The water will be over us soon.

WENDY

We have to go.

PETER

Wendy, I can't.

WENDY

You're bleeding.

PETER

Hook cut me.

WENDY

Fly Peter.

PETER

I can't fly.

WENDY

Swim.

PETER

I can't. I'm too weak.

WENDY

Look, the water's rising! We'll drown.

(Suddenly a kite floats over the sea to Peter and Wendy.)

PETER

A kite! Look, it's Tootles' kite! It flew away. It lifted him off
the ground. It'll carry you.

WENDY

Both of us!

PETER

No. It can't lift two.

WENDY

I won't go without you.

PETER

You have to. The water's rising.

WENDY

No. I'm not leaving you.

*(Peter ties the kite tail around Wendy. She clings
to him, refusing to go without him. They
struggle. He pushes her off. She floats up.)*

WENDY

No, no!

PETER

Goodbye, Wendy.

*(Wendy flies away lifted by the kite. Peter is
alone on the lagoon. The rock is very small now.
Soon it will be submerged. Peter is bleeding. The
world gets very dark and even more dangerous.
Pale rays of light tiptoe across the waters.
Sound of a drumbeat. As if we hear Peter's
heartbeat.)*

To die will be an awfully big adventure.

LOST BOYS/WENDY/JOHN (SING.)

No more haunting dreams,
No shadows on the wall,
No more baby screams,
Just hear the fairy call:
"Come away, come away, come away…"

Come away, Oh human child!
To the waters and the wild.
With a fairy, hand in hand,
For the world's more full of weeping than you can
understand.

No more mothers cries
Just wash away your fears
Stars sing lullabies
They whisper in your ears:
"Come away, come away, come away…"

Come away, Oh human child!
To the waters and the wild.

LOST BOYS/WENDY/JOHN (SING.) (CONT)
With a fairy, hand in hand,
For the world's more full of weeping than you can understand.
"Come away, come away, come away…"

(The boys and Wendy gather around Peter's lifeless body. Peter wakes up. He's alive! He stands up and crows. Blackout.)

<u>END OF ACT ONE</u>

ACT TWO

12. THE HOME UNDER THE GROUND

(The lost boys shimmy down several ropes onto the ground. During the following, they set up the house bit by bit. It's like children playing make-believe if the make-believe were real. There is a random logic to this architecture – fully understood by the children. They attach the nursery furniture, random objects and toys to rope and hoist them up to the ceiling– like building a fort when you're a kid. Everything dangles over their heads and they play below. The mattresses and pillows remain on the floor. They wrap string around all the objects. The boys fish in a hole in the floor. Wendy stretches string and hangs up the washing to dry. The boys fight and play games.)

LOST BOYS (CHANT.)

Down... Down... Down... Down...
Don't blink twice for you have found
Where lost boys rule and pirates drown,
Where the outside world's turned upside down
In the home under the ground.

JOHN

The Lost Boys lived very happily in their home under the ground. Entrance to the home under the ground was by way of several large trees, each with a hole in its hollow trunk as large as a boy.

JOHN (CONT)

But there was one recess in the wall, no larger than a bird-cage, which was the private apartment of Tinker Bell. No woman, however large, could have had a more exquisite boudoir and bed-chamber combined. There was a chandelier from Tiddlywinks for the look of the thing, but of course she lit the residence herself. Their home was rough and simple, and not unlike what baby bears would have made of an underground house in the same circumstances.

(All the children sip imaginary tea from imaginary teacups on the floor. A game of make-believe. Commotion.)

WENDY

(Playing Mother.) Silence. You mustn't all talk at once. Is your mug empty, Slightly darling?

SLIGHTLY

(Play acting.) Not quite empty, Mother, thank you.

NIBS

(Play acting.) Mummy, He hasn't even begun to drink his milk.

SLIGHTLY

I complain of Nibs!

(John raises his hand.)

WENDY

Well, John?

JOHN
May I sit in father's chair, as he's not here?

WENDY
Sit in father's chair? Certainly not.

NIBS
I complain of John!

TOOTLES
I don't suppose that I could be father.

WENDY
No, Tootles.

TOOTLES
As I can't be father, I don't suppose I could be Mother?

WENDY
I'm sorry Tootles, no.

TOOTLES
As I can't be anything important, would any of you like to
see me do a trick?

ALL
No!

TOOTLES
I hadn't really any hope.

NIBS
Slightly is coughing on the table.

SLIGHTLY
Nibs is taking both butter and honey.

TOOTLES

(With his mouth full.) Tootles is speaking with his mouth full.
Oh. I am Tootles, aren't I?

NIBS

I complain of Slightly.

SLIGHTLY

I complain of Nibs.

TOOTLES

I complain of Tootles. Oh, I did it again!

WENDY

Children, children, children, tea is finished. Go outside and
play.

(The lost boys exit. John and Wendy alone.)

JOHN

Mother, Can you tell us a story before bedtime?

WENDY

John, You can call me Wendy. We're not playing pretend
right now.

JOHN

Why would I call you that, Mother?

WENDY

Wendy.

JOHN

Mother.

WENDY

Wendy.

JOHN

Mother.

WENDY

John, It's Wendy. I'm not your Mother, I'm your sister. Don't you remember?

JOHN

Oh, of course I do. Wendy. I'm sorry. It's just all rather confusing.

WENDY

John, Neverland is full of forgetting, but we can never forget our real life and our real mother.

JOHN

I am forgetting her. I'm forgetting everything.

WENDY

You must remember, John.

JOHN

Some things I don't want to remember, Wendy.

WENDY

What color were Mother's eyes?

JOHN

I don't remember.

WENDY

Was Mother blonde or brunette?

JOHN

I don't remember.

WENDY

What did Mother used to say when we were being naughty?

JOHN

I don't remember.

WENDY

Do you remember Mother's party dress? Or her laugh? Or her stories? Or the way she would tuck us in at night? Do you remember Michael? John, I know it's getting much harder to tell when you're asleep or awake but that's the game. You must always remember what is real and what is make-believe.

JOHN

Mother's eyes were brown, Wendy. They were brown.

> *(Sound of Peter crowing upstairs. The boys enter.)*

WENDY

Time for the game again, John.

> *(Peter enters.)*

PETER

(Playing Father.) Hello children!

LOST BOYS

Hello Father!

PETER

The Indians are now our allies.

WENDY

That's wonderful Father.

SLIGHTLY

Any sport, Father?

PETER

Two tigers and a pirate.

NIBS

Where are their heads?

PETER

In the bag.

(Lost boys peep into the bag.)

PETER

Ah, Mother, there is nothing more pleasant of an evening for you and me when the day's toil is over than to rest by the fire with the little ones nearby.

WENDY

It is sweet, father, isn't it? I think Nibs has your nose. Slightly have your eyelashes.

PETER

Tootles has your toenails.

(The boys play and horse around. They have a pillow fight.)

WENDY

It's time for bed, children.

LOST BOYS

No! No!

WENDY

Yes, It's time for bed, children.

LOST BOYS

No! No!

WENDY

Yes, it's time for bed.

LOST BOYS

No! No! No! No!

PETER

(Screams.) Go to sleep you stupid children!

(Silence. The boys get ready for bed.)

WENDY

Peter, what is it?

PETER

Wendy, it's only make-believe, isn't it, that I'm their father?

WENDY

Yes.

PETER

Because I would be so old if I was their real father.

WENDY

But they are ours, Peter, yours and mine.

PETER

But not really, Wendy?

WENDY

No. Not really. Not if you don't wish for it.

PETER

I don't.

WENDY

Peter, what are your exact feelings for me?

                    PETER

Those of a son, Wendy.

                    WENDY

Nothing more?

                    PETER

What could be more?

                    WENDY

What did you say?

                    PETER

What could be more?

                    TOOTLES

Will you tell us a story, mother?

                    LOST BOYS

We want a story, a story!

                    WENDY

All right, a story.

13. WENDY'S STORY

*(All the boys except Peter get in the bed with
Wendy like sardines in a tin. Peter watches from
the corner of the room, apart from the group.)*

                    WENDY

Listen then, there once was a Lady –

                    NIBS

I wish it had been a white rat.

WENDY

Quiet. There once was a lady, and -

TOOTLES

Oh, mummy, you mean that there IS a lady, don't you? Not there ONCE WAS a lady? She's not dead, is she?

WENDY

Oh, no.

TOOTLES

I'm awfully glad she isn't dead. Aren't you glad, Slightly?

SLIGHTLY

Of course I am.

TOOTLES

Aren't you glad, Nibs?

NIBS

Rather.

WENDY

Oh dear. The Lady's name was Mrs. Darling.

JOHN

I think I knew her.

WENDY

And what do you think she had?

NIBS

White rats.

WENDY

No.

TOOTLES

Ooh, It's awfully puzzling.

WENDY

She had three descendants.

NIBS

What are descendants?

WENDY

Well, you are one, Nibs.

NIBS

Did you hear that, slightly? I am a descendant.

SLIGHTLY

Descendants are only children.

WENDY

Everyone is a descendant of someone, Nibs. Even white rats.
Now these three children lived very happily and played the
most wonderful games of make-believe until the littlest one,
Michael, fell asleep, and he never woke up.

TOOTLES

He never woke up? That's horrible.

WENDY

Then one night Peter Pan came and the other two children
flew away with him.

NIBS

It's an awfully good story.

WENDY

They flew away to Neverland, where the lost boys are.

SLIGHTLY

I just knew they did. I don't know how, but I just knew they
did!

TOOTLES

Oh Mother, was one of the lost boys called Tootles?

WENDY

Yes, he was.

TOOTLES

I'm in a story. Hurray! Slightly, I'm in a story.

WENDY

Now I want you to consider the feelings of the unhappy
Mother with her children flown away. Who was there to look
after her?

NIBS

But children aren't supposed to look after their mothers.
Mothers are supposed to look after their children.

WENDY

That's right, Nibs. Think of the empty beds!

TOOTLES

It's awfully sad. I don't see how it can have a happy ending.
I'm frightfully anxious.

WENDY

If you knew how great a mother's love is, you would have no
fear.

TOOTLES

I do like a mother's love. Do you like a mother's love,
Slightly?

SLIGHTLY

I just do. *(Hits Tootles.)*

WENDY

You see, our heroine knew that her mother would always leave the window open for her children to fly back. So they stayed away for moons and moons and had the most amazing adventures.

JOHN

I imagine the mother missed them very much. Did the children ever go back?

WENDY

Let us now take a peep into the future. Years have rolled by, and who is this elegant lady of uncertain age alighting at London Station?

NIBS

Oh Mother, who is she?

WENDY

Can it be - yes - no – yes - it is the fair Wendy!

TOOTLES

I am glad.

WENDY

And who is the noble portly figure accompanying her, now grown up to be a man? Can that be John? It is! And look! Their nursery window is still left open. Who could ever lose faith in a mother's love? So up they flew to their mother, and there they lived happily ever after.

PETER

Wendy, You're wrong about mothers. ...Long ago, I thought
like you that my mother would always keep the window
open for me, so I stayed away for moons and moons, and
then I flew back. But the window was locked. My mother
had forgotten all about me. And there was another little boy
sleeping in my bed. Mothers are horrible people. I hate them.
...And that is the truth about mothers.

TOOTLES

Are you sure mothers are like that?

JOHN

That's not true.

PETER

Yes it is. Wendy, remember I told you every time you take a
breath in Neverland a grown up dies? *(He takes a big
breath.)* I hope your mother just died.

JOHN

Wendy, let's go home.

WENDY

Yes.

TOOTLES

No.

SLIGHTLY

Not tonight?

WENDY

At once. My mother is very much alive, I know it, but she
must be in half-mourning for us by now. We have to go
home. Peter, will you make the necessary arrangements?

PETER

If you wish.

WENDY

Thank you, Peter.

PETER

Tinker Bell will take you across the sea. Wake her, Nibs.

(Nibs knocks on Tinker Bell's apartment.)

NIBS

You are to get up, think, and take Wendy on a journey.

(Tinker Bell responds.)

She says she won't.

PETER

Tinker Bell!

(Tinker Bell responds.)
She will.

WENDY

Dear ones, if you will all come with me I feel almost sure I can get my mother to adopt you.

TOOTLES

But won't she think of us rather a handful?

WENDY

Oh no, I can't imagine. It will only mean having a few more beds in the nursery.

LOST BOYS

Peter, can we go?

PETER

Fine.

WENDY

But first, everyone must take his medicine before you go.

*(She gets out the medicine bottle and spoon.
Wendy pours medicine and gives it to each boy.)*

All right, now get your things. We're going home.

WENDY

Peter, here's your medicine.

PETER

I'm not going Wendy.

WENDY

Yes, Peter.

PETER

No.

WENDY

Come home with me, and my mother could be your mother.

PETER

Would she send me to school?

WENDY

Yes.

PETER

And then to an office?

WENDY

I suppose so.

PETER

I don't want to go to school and learn stupid things. I don't want to be a man. I want to always be a little boy and to have fun.

WENDY

But, Peter -

PETER

Wendy, I would die if I were to wake up one day and feel a beard on my face.

WENDY

Peter, I should love you with a beard. *(Wendy touches his face.)*

PETER

Is this what you want? *(He kisses her.)* This? *(He kisses her again.)* More? *(He kisses her again.)* There. Take a hundred thimbles. *(Kisses her again.)* You want me to be a man? I'm not a man. You can never make me one. *(He pushes her away.)*

JOHN

Stop it. Leave her alone.

PETER

And you. You're not a lost boy. You're not brave. You're a scared little girl. You're nothing. Leave. Both of you. Grow up. What do I care about? You don't belong here. Get out of Neverland. Now. Go home to your stupid beds and go to sleep forever. Grow up and die.

WENDY

You don't mean that Peter.

PETER

Yes I do. Unlike grownups I mean every word I say.

WENDY

Peter, please. I want you to come. What are you so afraid of?

PETER

No. No one is ever going to catch me and make me a man.

WENDY

Come with me Peter. Please.

PETER

I can never grow up. Why can't you understand that?

WENDY

Please, Peter.

PETER

No.

WENDY

But, who will tuck you in at night, and hold you when you're having your nightmares? Peter, you need a mother.

PETER

You're my mother.

WENDY

No Peter, I'm not. I'm just a little girl. This is make-believe. And this medicine isn't real. Everyone saw me pouring it from the bottle. See? It's not real. None of it is. It's all make-believe. All of it. You. Me. This. Everyone knows it. You're the only one who doesn't.

PETER

Goodbye Wendy. Goodbye boys. If you find your mothers, I hope you like them. Are you ready, Tinker Bell? Lead the way.

*(The children start to leave and suddenly there's
the sound from above of a battle between the
Pirates and the Indians. Shrieks and the clash of
steel.)*

SLIGHTLY
The Pirates and the Indians are fighting!

*(Everything stops. Hook is above the house and
listens below. The children listen but can't see
him.)*

PETER
It's done.

JOHN
Who has won?

PETER
If the Indians have won, they'll beat the tom-tom. It's their
signal of victory.

*(Hook appears above and beats tom-tom with
his hook.)*

JOHN
Tom-tom!

NIBS
An Indian victory.

PETER
You're safe now, Wendy. Goodbye boys.

WENDY
Peter, thank you. You will remember to take your medicine?

PETER

It's not all just make-believe?

WENDY

No, it's not.

PETER

I'll take my medicine.

WENDY

Promise?

PETER

Yes.

WENDY

Goodbye Peter.

(The children climb up. Shadows above.)

14. THE DEATH AND RESURRECTION OF TINKER BELL

(Peter goes to sleep on the mattress.)

SLIGHTLY

Sometimes, though not often, Peter had dreams, and they were more painful than the dreams of other boys. For hours he could not be separated from these dreams, though he wailed piteously in them. They had to do, I think, with the riddle of his existence.

(Hook squeezes down a tree – He can't fit through the tree door to the home. He tries to reach Peter with his Hook. He can't. He watches Peter sleep.)

HOOK

Little boy, you have no idea the feelings you stir in me.

> *(Hook puts poison into Peter's medicine. He climbs back up through the tree. Silence.)*

PETER

(Waking up.) Wendy... Wendy... Who's that? What is it? Tink. The Indians were defeated? Wendy and the boys captured by the pirates! I'll save them! - Oh, that's just my medicine. Poisoned? Who could have poisoned it? No, I promised Wendy I'd take it.

> *(Tinker Bell drinks the poison.)*

Why, Tink, how dare you drink my medicine! You stupid fairy.

> *(Tink flutters around the room.)*

It was poisoned and you drank it to save my life. Tink. Tink, are you dying?

> *(She falls. Everything gets very dark.)*

Your light is going out. If it goes out, you die.

> *(All the lights go out. All of them.)*

No. Tink, are you dead?...

Maybe you'd come back if children believed in fairies.

> *(Peter addresses the audience. Like a prayer. Not a command, but a plea, quietly. He talks to us directly in the dark.)*

I address all of you who might be dreaming of the
Neverland. I am nearer to you than you think. Boys and girls
in your nighties, and babies in your baskets hung from trees,
all children who are dreaming now or have ever dreamed.
Do you believe in fairies? If you do, say that you believe.

> *(The other children enter in the darkness and
> slowly begin repeating: "I do believe in fairies"
> until Tinker Bell comes back to life.)*

You're alive! Oh, thank you, thank you, thank you. And now
to rescue Wendy. Hook, it's you or me this time!

> *(He crows. Peter and Tinker Bell fly off to rescue
> Wendy and the boys.)*

<u>15. THE PIRATE SHIP</u>

> *(The sea – dark waters - stars. A huge mast of a
> ship emerges. Ropes. Different parts of the Jolly
> Roger. The nursery creaks. During the following,
> Slightly plays with the toy pirate ship. Hook
> pushes the baby carriage. Hook opens Michael's
> grave.)*

SLIGHTLY

One green light squinting over Kidd's Creek, which is near
the mouth of the pirate river, marked where the brig, the
Jolly Roger, lay, low in the water; a rakish-looking craft foul
to the hull, every beam in her detestable, like ground strewn
with mangled feathers. She was the cannibal of the seas, and
scarcely needed that watchful eye, for she floated immune in
the horror of her name. She was wrapped in the blanket of
night, through which no sound from her could have reached
the shore. The ship was as monstrous as her captain.

(Hook is alone on the deck of the ship.)

HOOK

How still the night is. Nothing sounds alive. Now is the hour
when children, back from a night at the theatre, are in their
homes in bed. Their lips bright-browned with the goodnight
chocolate, and their tongues drowsily searching for belated
crumbs housed insecurely in their shining cheeks. Pan is
dead. Soon everything will be dead. A holocaust of
children...

> *(Smee brings the tied up children on and hoists
> them onto the deck. The children scream.)*

Quiet, you scags, or I'll pluck out your eyeballs! Now then
my little piggies, tonight you shall walk the plank! But, I do
have room for a cabin boy. Which of you is it to be? *(To
John.)* You, boy, you look as if you had a little pluck in you.
You have a pirate's mouth. Didst never want to be a pirate,
boy?

JOHN

Not really, no.

HOOK

Bring up the little mother.

> *(Wendy is driven up from the hold and thrown to
> him.)*

So, my beauty, you are to see your spawn walk the plank.

WENDY

Are they to die?

HOOK

Smart girl. They are to die. Just like your precious Peter.

WENDY

Peter.

HOOK

Oh yes, Pan's dead. Did I forget to mention it?

WENDY

No.

HOOK

Yes.

WENDY

I don't believe it.

HOOK

Believe it. Poisoned. I put it in his medicine myself. I know a
good mother always makes certain her children take their
medicine. And I know what a good mother you are. And
now, I shall give you the pleasure of watching the rest of
your piggies die. Silence all, for a mother's last words to her
children.

WENDY

Back at home, before Michael died, we would play at the
Neverland, and it was always fun. Sometimes it got dark by
bedtime. The shadows would rise on the nursery wall. I was
quite glad that the nightlights were on. And Mother would
remind me that that was just the rocking horse over there,
and the crib... and that the Neverland was all make-believe.
But now it's all quite different. It's real now, and there are no
nightlights, and it gets darker every day, and it doesn't look
like we can win. But, this is when I think we must believe
the most. I wish I had better words for you. If we are to die,
let us all die for Peter Pan!

LOST BOYS

For Peter! For Peter Pan!

HOOK

You horrid little girl! I'll kill them all!

> *(Wendy is roped to the mast. The plank is protruding over the ship's side. Suddenly, the sound of a ticking clock. Shadows. Peter is circling the ship. He drops into the water and climbs aboard, signaling to the captives.)*

HOOK

The clock. The clock. The crocodile! The Crocodile! Hide me!

> *(The ticking sound stops.)*

SMEE

It's gone, captain. The night is still again.

HOOK

Then here's to Johnny Plank! Do you want a touch of the cat before you walk the plank?

LOST BOYS

No, no!

> *(The shadow of the crocodile appears. Ticking sound.)*

HOOK

The crocodile! The crocodile!

> *(The ticking sound stops again.)*

SMEE

It's gone. It's a spirit, Captain. The ship is doomed!

HOOK

There's a Jonah aboard.

SMEE

Ay, a man with a hook.

HOOK

What did you say?

SMEE

Nothing, Captain.

HOOK

It's the girl. Never was luck on a pirate ship with a woman on board. We'll right the ship once she's gone. Fling the girl overboard.

SMEE

No.

HOOK

What did you say, Smee?

SMEE

No, Captain. Not the mother.

HOOK

Shut up you sniveling, weaselly little housewife. You pathetic piece of puce puss.

SMEE

They're only children.

HOOK

That is why they must die! Everyone grows up and everyone dies. All of you will die. You are already dying. You die a little everyday. You die with every breath you take. You're dying now. Die! Die! Die!

(Hook sticks his sword in Smee.)

SMEE

Mummy.

> *(Hook kills Smee. Hook takes Wendy to the plank.)*

HOOK

There's none can save you now, little mother.

WENDY

There's one.

HOOK

Who's that?

> *(Peter appears.)*

PETER

Peter Pan! *(He crows.)*

HOOK

Pan! No, Pan! You're dead! It's your shadow!

PETER

I'm alive!

HOOK

You're a ghost!

PETER

I'm a boy!

> *(Tinker Bell unties the children. Slightly takes Smee's sword. The boys advance on Hook.)*

HOOK

I'll show you the road to dusty death. Back, you pewling spawn!

PETER

Put up your swords, boys. This man is mine.

(The boys back down. Pan and Hook face off.)

HOOK

Proud and insolent youth, prepare to meet thy doom.

PETER

Dark and sinister man, have at thee.

(They begin. It's a spectacular sword fight. The one we've been waiting for at last. Peter flies around Hook and they fight all over the ship.)

HOOK

'Tis some fiend fighting me! Pan, who and what art thou?

PETER

I'm youth. I'm joy. I'm a little bird just cracked out of the egg. I'm kicking and screaming. I'm young and you're old. I'm alive and you're dead. I'm a kite in the sky. I'm a flame, a comet, a thunderstorm! I'm a thousand children laughing!

HOOK

I'll be the death of you, boy!

PETER

I'm the waves, the rain, a flock of birds! I'm a play that's just begun! I'm magic! I'm make-believe! I'm theatre! I'm alive!

(They move the sword fight to the plank. Hook disarms Peter and presses his sword to his throat.)

HOOK

I'm going to tell you a secret now, boy. We're the same, you and I. Only you're at the beginning and I'm at the end. I'm somewhere deep inside of you. I'm the shadow that frightens you the most. I'm the voice that wakes you up at night and whispers: "I'm coming for you. I'm coming... I'm close... I'm here..." I'm your worst fear. And you will never get rid of me Peter, because I'm *you*. I'm you all grown up.

PETER

I'll never be you. Never. Go ahead. Kill me. Kill me.

> *(Hook raises his sword. Sound of a clock ticking – but this time it's the real crocodile - in the sea right below the plank.)*

HOOK

No! No! That sound! I'm going mad!

> *(Peter grabs his sword and they sword fight more – Peter gets the advantage. He backs Hook to the very edge of the plank - dangling just above the crocodile in the sea below.)*

Peter Pan, boy who haunts my dreams, how I hate you.

> *(Peter cuts Hook's hook off of him and pushes him off the plank in the water into the mouth of the crocodile.)*

Ahhhhhhh!

PETER

Thus perished James Hook.

*(The children cheer. They celebrate. The ship
sets sail with Peter as captain and the boys as
crew.)*

TOOTLES

The ship set sail. Peter had one of his dreams that night, and
cried in his sleep for a long time, and Wendy held him
tightly.

*(During the following, the children transform
the nursery back to its original state.)*

WENDY

It is the nightly custom of every good mother after her
children are asleep to rummage in their minds and put things
straight for next morning, repacking into their proper places
the many articles that have wandered during the day. If you
could keep awake - but of course you can't - you would see
your own mother doing this, and you would find it very
interesting to watch her. It is quite like tidying up drawers.

You would see her on her knees, I expect, lingering
humorously over some of your contents, wondering where
on earth you had picked this thing up, making discoveries
sweet and not so sweet, pressing this to her cheek as if it
were as nice as a kitten, and hurriedly stowing that out of
sight. When you wake in the morning, the naughtiness and
evil passions with which you went to bed have been folded
up small and placed at the bottom of your mind and on the
top, beautifully aired, are spread out your prettier thoughts,
ready for you to put on.

16. THE RETURN HOME

TOOTLES

We must now return to that desolate home from which Wendy and John had taken heartless flight so long ago. It seems a shame to have neglected it all this time, and yet we may be sure that Mrs. Darling does not blame us. She was in the nursery, a very sad-eyed woman. Look at her in her chair, where she has fallen asleep. The corner of her mouth, where one looks first, is almost withered up. Her hand moves restlessly on her breast as if she had a pain there. Some like Peter best, and some like Wendy best, but I like her best.

(Peter flies in through the nursery window. Mrs. Darling and Peter alone. Peter pulls a knife on Mrs. Darling. Beat. He goes to her, touches her face and hair gently. He flies out. Wendy and John fly in the open window and into the nursery.)

JOHN

Wendy, I believe I've been here before in my dreams.

WENDY

This is where we used to live.

JOHN

Is that her?

WENDY

Yes. Let's slip into our beds, and be there when she awakes, just as if we had never been away.

*(Wendy and John get into their beds. Mrs.
Darling wakes. She sees the children asleep in
their beds, but she doesn't believe they're there.)*

MRS. DARLING

I see you in your beds so often in my dreams that I
sometimes see you still when I'm awake.

WENDY

You're not dreaming Mother.

MRS. DARLING

...Wendy? ...John?

(They embrace. Peter appears at the window.)

PETER

Wendy.

*(Mrs. Darling pulls her children away from
him.)*

WENDY

Mother, this is Peter.

MRS. DARLING

...You've come to take him, haven't you?

*(Peter nods. He goes to the floorboards where
baby Michael is buried, pulls up the floorboards
and digs him up. He picks baby Michael up,
holds him in his arms and carries him to the
window.)*

WENDY

I'll come with you.

MRS. DARLING

No.

WENDY

But he does so need a mother.

MRS. DARLING

So do you, my love.

WENDY

But mother, I couldn't bear to never see him again.

MRS. DARLING

I shall let her go to you once a year for a week in the spring,
if you promise to bring her back.

WENDY

Oh, thank you Mother, thank you. You won't forget me,
Peter, will you, before the spring comes?

PETER

I promise.

*(Peter kisses Mrs. Darling. He flies away with
the baby.)*

SLIGHTLY

And then he flew away. He took Mrs. Darling's kiss with
him. The kiss that had been for no one else, Peter took quite
easily.

17. EVERYONE GROWS UP

SLIGHTLY

Of course all the lost boys went to live with Mrs. Darling as well. At first, she tied their feet to the bedposts so that they should not fly away in the night. In time they could not even fly after their hats. Want of practice, they called it, but what it really meant was that they no longer believed.

TOOTLES

Tootles believed longer than the other boys, though they jeered at him. Peter flew back, just as he'd promised, the following year.

(Peter flies in through the window.)

PETER

Wendy, I just killed a dozen pirates!

WENDY

Oh, how thrilling. Was it like the night you killed Captain Hook?

PETER

Who's Captain Hook?

WENDY

Captain Hook. Don't you remember how you killed him and saved all our lives?

PETER

I forget them after I kill them.

WENDY

Did Tink come with you?

PETER

Tink?

WENDY

Tinker Bell.

PETER

Who is Tinker Bell?

WENDY

Oh, Peter. She's your fairy.

PETER

There are such a lot of them. Maybe she died.

NIBS

Fairies don't live long, but they are so little that a short time seems a good while to them. Wendy was pained to find that the past year was but as yesterday to Peter. It had seemed such a long year of waiting to her.

TOOTLES

The next year he did not come for her. She waited in a new frock because the old one simply would not meet. But he never came.

(Wendy is waiting by the window with John.)

JOHN

Perhaps he's ill.

WENDY

You know he is never ill.

JOHN

Perhaps he never existed, Wendy.

TOOTLES

Peter came the next spring, and the strange thing was that he never knew he had missed a year.

(Peter flies in and goes to Wendy. He whispers a secret in her ear and flies away.)

WENDY

That was the last time the girl Wendy ever saw him.

(Adult Wendy enters.)

ADULT WENDY/WENDY

The years came and went without bringing the careless boy,

WENDY

And when they met again Wendy was a married woman,

ADULT WENDY

And Peter was no more to her than a little dust in the box in which she had kept her toys.

ALL

All children grow up.

ADULT WENDY

Except one. ...Wendy grew up. You need not be sorry for her. She was one of the kind that likes to grow up. In the end she grew up of her own free will a day quicker than other girls.

NIBS

All the boys grew up as well. You may see Nibs any day going to an office, carrying a little bag and an umbrella.

SLIGHTLY

Slightly married a lady of title, and so he became a lord.

TOOTLES

You see that old drunk coming out of the alley? That used to be Tootles.

JOHN

The bearded man who doesn't know any story to tell his children was once John.

ADULT WENDY

Wendy was married in white with a pink sash. Years rolled on again, and Wendy had a daughter. This ought not to be written in ink but in a golden splash.

TOOTLES

And then one night came the tragedy.

> *(Jane is asleep in the bed. Adult Wendy is asleep in a chair. It's dark. The window blows open and Peter drops in on the floor. He is exactly the same as ever. He is a little boy, and she is grown up.)*

PETER

Hello, Wendy.

ADULT WENDY

Hello, Peter. Are you expecting me to fly away with you?

PETER

Of course. Come away!

ADULT WENDY

I can't. I've forgotten how to fly.

PETER

I'll teach you again.

ADULT WENDY

Peter, don't waste the fairy dust on me.

PETER

What is it?

102

ADULT WENDY

I'll turn on the light, and you can see for yourself.

PETER

Wendy, don't turn on the light.

> *(She lets her hands play in the hair of the tragic boy. They kiss in the dark. She is not a little girl heart-broken about him; she is a grown woman smiling at it all, but they are wet eyed smiles. She turns up the light, and Peter sees her.)*

What is it?

ADULT WENDY

I'm old Peter. I'm ever so much more than twenty. I grew up long ago.

PETER

You promised not to.

ADULT WENDY

I couldn't help it. I'm a married woman, Peter.

PETER

No, you're not.

ADULT WENDY

Yes, and the little girl in the bed is my baby.

PETER

No, she's not.

ADULT WENDY

Yes, I'm her mother.

PETER

No. You promised.

ADULT WENDY

I'm sorry, Peter.

> *(Adult Wendy rushes from the room. Peter sits down on the floor and cries. Jane wakes up.)*

JANE

Boy, why are you crying?

PETER

Hello.

JANE

Hello.

PETER

My name is Peter Pan.

JANE

Yes, I know. My mother told me about you. I've been waiting for you.

PETER

Will you be my mother?

JANE

I will.

> *(Adult Wendy appears in the doorway.)*

ADULT WENDY

Peter.

PETER

She'll be my mother now.

ADULT WENDY

No.

JANE

He does so need a mother.

ADULT WENDY

Yes, I know. No one knows it so well as I.

PETER

Goodbye Wendy.

(Peter and Jane go to the window.)

ADULT WENDY

Please. If only I could go with you.

PETER

You can't fly.

(Peter and Jane fly out the window into the night sky.)

JANE

Of course in the end Wendy let them fly away together. Our last glimpse of her shows her at the window, watching them receding into the sky until they were as small as stars. As you look at Wendy, you may see her hair becoming white, and her figure little again, for all this happened long ago.

ADULT WENDY

Jane became a grownup, with a daughter called Margaret, and every spring, except when he forgot, Peter came for Margaret and took her to the Neverland, where she told him stories about himself, to which he listened eagerly. When Margaret grew up she had a daughter, who was Peter's mother in turn, and she will have a daughter too.
And thus it will go on, and on, and on, so long as children are gay and innocent and heartless.

<u>END OF PLAY</u>

www.ingramcontent.com/pod-product-compliance
Lightning Source LLC
Chambersburg PA
CBHW022107050726

47591CB00002B/710